BIRD OF THE SOUL

ALSO BY ILCHI LEE

Change

The Call of Sedona

Healing Society

The Twelve Enlightenments for Healing Society

Brain Wave Vibration

In Full Bloom

Principles of Brain Management

Healing Chakras

Mago's Dream

Human Technology

LifeParticle Meditation

Bird
of the Soul

ILCHI LEE

Illustrated by JISU HAN

BEST
LIFE
MEDIA

Best Life Media
6560 State Route 179, Suite 114
Sedona, AZ 86351
www.bestlifemedia.com
877-504-1106

First hardcover edition: January 2014
Revised hardcover edition: May 2014
Library of Congress Control Number: 2013957403
ISBN-13: 978-1-935127-68-0

Music Permission Acknowledgments
Track 1 on the CD: One Fine Spring Day by Isao Sasaki
Track 2 on the CD: Nella Fantasia, written by Ennio Morricone and Chiara Rerrau, sung by Sarah Brightman, licensing arranged by HFA

Cover and interior design by Malou Leontsinis. Illustrations by Jisu Han.

To all the beautiful people who seek
to genuinely love themselves
and to live the life their souls truly want.

AUTHOR'S INTRODUCTION

Some people doubt the existence of the soul. I think this must be because they have little experience with it. In everyday life, a cacophony of thoughts and emotions drowns out the voice of the soul so it can no longer be heard. And with time, the existence of the soul may be completely forgotten.

Yet, I'm certain we are all precious beings with souls, not just visible bodies. Perhaps that's why even those who doubt the existence of the soul feel pretty bad when they hear someone say, "You have no soul." Everyone yearns to connect with something more permanent and meaningful than what ordinary life offers.

That's why I've created Bird of the Soul Training—to help people easily feel close to their soul. I've already enabled people to experience this through workshops, and this book and training CD is designed to bring this experience into your home. Visualizing the Bird of the Soul, which represents the energy of the soul in our hearts, allows a concrete, vivid connection to the soul.

Our souls want to be free, like birds soaring in the blue sky. Yet heavy emotions from past memories, attachments, and fixed beliefs often weigh them down, keeping them from flying free. We feel stuck, like a butterfly caught in a spider's web. For our souls to be free, we need to purify our heavy, tangled emotions and to embrace pure, emotion-free energy.

No matter how difficult your life has been, you can be certain that your soul is still in perfect condition, waiting for you to set it free. Sometimes you may feel so heavy-hearted that it seems as if your soul has left you, but this is never the case. The soul, by its very nature, cannot be corrupted, cannot be hurt, and cannot be destroyed. If it feels otherwise, it is merely because your soul has become hidden behind layers of negative life experiences. But these are merely an outer shell surrounding the soul; the soul itself is always pure and whole.

In life, we chase after things like money and status, but these things have no lasting value relative to the soul. Only the soul has absolute value, which is why I believe it should be at the center of everyone's life. Human societies are full of separations and boundaries, but the soul is beyond all of that. Through our souls we can connect to what I call the LifeParticle Sun—the universe's expression of total oneness and absolute brightness. As we connect to this, we connect to the vibrant root of life itself, which is also the root of the soul. All difficult emotions fall away instantly when we reconnect with the soul, and we are transported to a timeless realm beyond the petty concerns of this world.

Through its beautiful, playful illustrations, this book tells the story of Jay, a man who resembles many of us who have become distanced from their souls through the years. Like Jay, you can recover the feeling of being a pure, free soul, as you experienced when you were very young. I hope that as you travel life's journey with Jay, you will regain that which is very precious and important, that which you may have forgotten.

The CD included in the back of the book contains the Bird of the Soul guided meditation, comprising two audio tracks. The first meditation clears away heavy, unresolved emotions related to memories of negative experiences. A soul can only fly as free as a bird if the energy around it is light and pure, which this meditation will help you achieve. The second track guides you as you fly with the bird of your soul, enabling you to experience deeply your soul's freedom.

The 21-Day Meditation Journal, also found in the back of the book, may be used to develop your soul's energy as you meet and communicate with the bird of your soul for 21 days. Through 21 days of meditation, I hope your soul's energy will gradually expand, and your soul will finally take its place at the center of your life.

May your days be filled with the fresh fragrance of your soul.

January 2014, Sedona
Ilchi Lee

When Jay was born, the bird of his soul was born with him, and the bird built a nest in his heart.

Jay and his soul bird grew up together.
When Jay laughed, his soul bird laughed with him.
When Jay rejoiced, his soul bird rejoiced, too.

$\mathcal{E}$very day, Jay would sit under a giant elm tree and imagine the adventures his life might bring. Whenever he was lost in his imagination, his soul bird spread his wings and flew with him. Jay could become whatever he wanted when he was with the bird of his soul.

ometimes, however, Jay felt sad because he had been scolded or snubbed by the people around him. At these times, his soul bird felt sad, too. But the wise bird would take heart and sing Jay a song.

"Don't worry when the sky is dark.
The sun is always there.
Just wait and you will see it
When the clouds begin to clear.
The same is true when you feel alone,
Or it seems that life's unfair.
I always have been, always will be
Waiting for you here."

When Jay sang along with his soul bird,
he would feel happy again. He'd climb up into the branches
of the old elm tree and let his mind fly free.

The elm tree sang along with the bird's song,
and so did the warm sunshine and the gentle breeze.

"I always have been, always will be
Waiting for you here."

Time flew by, and Jay grew quickly.
He made many new friends at school,
and filled up his time with
homework and chores.
He went to the elm tree
less and less often,
until he stopped
going altogether.

He spent more time playing with his friends,
and less time with the bird of his soul,
who now spent more and more time alone.

Still, every time Jay's heart was wounded,
 the bird of his soul was hurt as well.
Yet, as always, the bird of his soul took heart and sang for Jay.

"Don't worry when the sky is dark.
The sun is always there.
Just wait and you will see it
When the clouds begin to clear.

The same is true when you feel alone
Or it seems that life's unfair.
I always have been, always will be
Waiting for you here."

But now Jay's mind was so full of other things that
he could no longer hear the bird's song.

Soon Jay grew up.

He got a job, got married, and started a family.

Now he had so many responsibilities to take care of!

Like all the other grownups,

he talked more of being busy than of being happy.

He completely forgot about the little bird

singing its beautiful song in his heart.

Jay never smiled anymore, even when the breeze tickled his face. His heart no longer fluttered when winter changed into spring. And, sadly, even when he gazed at the stars twinkling in the night sky, his mind no longer filled with wonder.

He had forgotten how to soar upon the wings of his soul to the edges of the universe, so his world now seemed very small.

Jay was unhappy.
Everything in his life felt heavy and hard.
And the unhappier he was,
the weaker the bird of his soul became.
With its wounded wings folded away,
it could no longer fly.

"My beloved Jay's forgotten me,
But I will always remember.
I hope one day that he will see
That I am with him forever."

*H*is bird cried, and a small hole appeared in Jay's heart.
The bird's tears didn't stop, and the hole got bigger and bigger.

Jay couldn't fill that empty space with anything.
Nothing brought him joy.
No one could make him happy.
He felt he had lost something very precious.

But what was it? He had no idea.

One day he asked a friend,
"Have you ever wondered if there could
be something more to life?"

Patting him on the shoulder, his friend replied,
"If you have people who love you and a good job,
isn't that enough?

You have a strong, healthy child and a wonderful wife.
What more is there to search for? You have a good life.
Isn't it better to be satisfied with what you have now,
than to desire something new that you may never achieve?
It's risky to have hopes and dreams without any guarantees."

Jay thought his friend might be right.
Yet he frequently woke up in the middle of the night,
staring at the ceiling, tossing and turning, unable to sleep.

One night, Jay had a dream.
In his dream he was walking, walking, walking
without any rest. But it was strange:
No matter how much he walked,
the scenery never changed.
On both sides, he kept seeing
the same houses and trees.
He'd been walking in place!
Working hard but going nowhere.

$\mathcal{W}$hen Jay awoke from his dream,
he felt an ache in his heart, and longed to fill the gaping hole
that seemed to bring only sadness and loneliness.
The pain was so great it was hard to breathe.

Suddenly he felt heat rise up in his chest,
and he found himself crying, tears rolling down his cheeks.
Jay was confused, and he couldn't hold back the tears.
Then he heard a faint voice coming from somewhere.

"It's okay to dream a dream that's better than today.
Let go now of your fear and remember that I am here."

Startled, Jay looked around, but saw nothing.
Again he heard the small voice calling:

"Now it's time to close your eyes
To see more than eyes can see.
If you look within your heart,
I am here, and you are free."

Jay closed his eyes and became quiet.
He tried to feel his heart, to look within his self.
And he saw the little bird.

"It's you! My little bird. Where have you been?"

"Yes, yes, it's me. The little bird of your soul.
I have always been here, and I always will be.
Oh Jay, how I've missed you!"

"Jay replied to the bird,
I'm sorry. I'm so sorry, my little bird.
I'm sorry for leaving you alone.
I'm sorry for hiding you away.
Only now do I realize how much I've missed you."

Jay caressed the bird. Its wings were weak and struggled to open.

"My little bird. How can we get you flying again?"

The soul bird said to Jay,
"All you have to do is give me strong wings.
Give me wings broader than the branches of the great elm tree,
So I can hold and heal your wounded heart.
Give me wings softer than a mother's smile,
So your mind can embrace the whole world with love.
Give me wings brighter than a rainbow,
So you can be happy even on a cloudy day."

"But how can I do that?"

The bird sang again,
"Plant hope's seed within your heart,
For hope's where happiness can start."

"But I lost all hope long ago," Jay said weakly.
"Without it, how can I give you new wings?"

"My beloved Jay, look into my eyes.
Look deeply, and a font of hope you'll find,
For you will remember the power of your mind.
If on the seas of life you're tossed,
I can restore the hope you've lost.

When your eyes and mine are aligned,
You're sure to meet your infinite and eternal mind.
I am here to make you complete and whole,
For I am your hope, your guide — your soul."

Jay looked into the bird's eyes,
and tears of joy came to his own.
The bird of his soul started singing more strongly.

"Now it is time to give me a name,
Knowing you and I are one and the same.
Look into your deepest heart
And surely we will never part.
Every time you call my name,
I'll fly to you and be your wings."

Jay thought for a moment.
"Hope! I will name you Hope!"
he exclaimed.
The soul bird's wings suddenly
spread as wide and strong
as the elm tree's branches.

"All right, now, shall we fly?" Jay asked Hope.
As if he had been waiting to hear those words,
Hope spread his wings.

"Are you ready?
On the count of three, let's soar into the sky together!
One! Two! Three!"

As one they flew high into the sky, soaring far and wide.
Smiles spread across their faces as bright and clear
as the dazzling sun rising above the horizon.

$\mathcal{B}$elow them, the flowers in the field glowed in their many colors and the lakes and rivers shimmered emerald in the sunlight. Jay's heart pounded with joy, and a warm breeze blew through his heart.

"I feel free!"
He shouted as he spread his arms wide.

Hope beat his broad, strong wings majestically
while he sang.

"Never again forget my name.
Far more dear than wealth or fame,
More important than being clever,
Keep me with you forever and ever.

I will love you all your days.
I will be with you always.

I am your hope.
I am your soul.

Call my name every day.
If you think of me and are with me,
The infinite power of your mind will never leave you."

Jay embraced the bird of his soul tightly.
Hope wrapped his shining wings around Jay.
Jay felt all his burdens fall away.

And, although sadness and struggle would
return, he would never again forget
the sweet song of the bird of his soul.

The guided meditation CD and 21-Day Meditation Journal in the back of this book are designed to help you reconnect with your soul.

I recommend that you practice the Bird of the Soul meditation for 21 days with the CD and write down your awakenings and inspirations in the journal after your meditation.

There are two tracks on the CD. The first is a meditation for feeling your soul and healing its wounds; the second is a meditation for experiencing your soul's freedom as you fly with your soul bird.

For your soul to fly free, you must first heal its wounds, making its energy brighter and lighter. So, at first, listen to tracks 1 and 2 in order and follow along with the meditation.

After you repeat this meditation several times and feel your energy is sufficiently purified and light, you can skip track 1 and practice only with track 2. At that time, before playing the track, sense your soul's energy in your heart as you feel your breath with your eyes closed. Additionally, when you fly with the bird of your soul in meditation, you could get up and do a free-style energy dance, if you wish.

Day 1

Congratulations today on your first meeting with the bird of your soul. Draw a picture or write a description below of the shape and colors of your soul bird as you saw it during the meditation. Also, give the bird of your soul a beautiful name.

What is the name of the bird of your soul?

_____

What did you feel today through your Bird of the Soul meditation?

_____

_____

_____

_____

_____

_____

_____

_____

_____

_____

_____

_____

_____

_____

_____

Day 2

What did you feel today through your Bird of the Soul meditation?

_____

_____

_____

_____

_____

_____

_____

_____

_____

_____

_____

_____

_____

_____

_____

_____

_____

Live a life in which you love and share the best in your soul. When you express the beauty of your soul sincerely and truthfully, you can be a bright light that shines on everyone.

What did you feel today through your Bird of the Soul meditation?

_____

_____

_____

_____

_____

_____

_____

_____

_____

_____

_____

_____

_____

_____

_____

_____

_____

Day 4

What did you feel today through your Bird of the Soul meditation?

_____

_____

_____

_____

_____

_____

_____

_____

_____

_____

_____

_____

_____

_____

_____

_____

Day 5

What did you feel today through your Bird of the Soul meditation?

_____

_____

_____

_____

_____

_____

_____

_____

_____

_____

_____

_____

_____

_____

_____

_____

_____

_____

_____

Day 6

*When you see the world through the eyes of your soul,
you witness the great, holy divinity and soul in the
hearts of all people, and you love and respect them.*

What did you feel today through your Bird of the Soul meditation?

_____

_____

_____

_____

_____

_____

_____

_____

_____

_____

_____

_____

_____

_____

_____

_____

Day 7

What did you feel today through your Bird of the Soul meditation?

_____

_____

_____

_____

_____

_____

_____

_____

_____

_____

_____

_____

_____

_____

_____

_____

_____

Day 8

What did you feel today through your Bird of the Soul meditation?

_____

_____

_____

_____

_____

_____

_____

_____

_____

_____

_____

_____

_____

_____

_____

_____

*The body is a means, a tool, and a musical instrument
by which the soul is expressed through vibration.*

What did you feel today through your Bird of the Soul meditation?

_____

_____

_____

_____

_____

_____

_____

_____

_____

_____

_____

_____

_____

_____

_____

Day 10

What did you feel today through your Bird of the Soul meditation?

_____

_____

_____

_____

_____

_____

_____

_____

_____

_____

_____

_____

_____

_____

_____

_____

_____

Day 11

Remain peaceful in your heart without attachment to others, and your soul will grow.

What did you feel today through your Bird of the Soul meditation?

_____

_____

_____

_____

_____

_____

_____

_____

_____

_____

_____

_____

_____

_____

_____

_____

Day 12

What did you feel today through your Bird of the Soul meditation?

_____

_____

_____

_____

_____

_____

_____

_____

_____

_____

_____

_____

_____

_____

_____

_____

_____

Day 13

What did you feel today through your Bird of the Soul meditation?

Day 14

By making choices for truth and keeping your
resolution in the face of challenges and desires, your
soul grows stronger and more mature.

What did you feel today through your Bird of the Soul meditation?

_____

_____

_____

_____

_____

_____

_____

_____

_____

_____

_____

_____

_____

_____

Day 15

What did you feel today through your Bird of the Soul meditation?

_____

_____

_____

_____

_____

_____

_____

_____

_____

_____

_____

_____

_____

_____

Day 16

What did you feel today through your Bird of the Soul meditation?

_____

_____

_____

_____

_____

_____

_____

_____

_____

_____

_____

_____

_____

_____

_____

_____

_____

Day 17

*Anyone who has a dream to make a new and
better world has a soul that is vibrant and free.
A free soul is love, joy, peace, and creation.*

What did you feel today through your Bird of the Soul meditation?

_____

_____

_____

_____

_____

_____

_____

_____

_____

_____

_____

_____

_____

_____

_____

_____

Day 18

What did you feel today through your Bird of the Soul meditation?

_____

_____

_____

_____

_____

_____

_____

_____

_____

_____

_____

_____

_____

_____

_____

_____

Day 19

Through your soul's awakening, you become able to choose and be master of your life.

What did you feel today through your Bird of the Soul meditation?

_____

_____

_____

_____

_____

_____

_____

_____

_____

_____

_____

_____

_____

_____

_____

_____

Day 20

What did you feel today through your Bird of the Soul meditation?

_____

_____

_____

_____

_____

_____

_____

_____

_____

_____

_____

_____

_____

_____

_____

_____

Day 21

What did you feel today through your Bird of the Soul meditation?

_____

_____

_____

_____

_____

_____

_____

_____

_____

_____

_____

_____

_____

_____

_____

_____

Congratulations

on completing a 21-day meditation with the bird of your soul. Draw a picture or write a description below of the shape and colors of your soul bird as you saw it during the meditation. How has your soul bird changed since you began the 21-day meditation?

As the clouds clear, the sun naturally shines. As your soul awakens, you start your soul journey toward completion.

What have you learned, and how have you grown during the past 21 days?

_____

_____

_____

_____

_____

_____

_____

_____

_____

_____

_____

_____

_____

_____

_____

_____

Acknowledgments

I would like to express my deep gratitude to Jisu Han for her illustrations that beautifully enliven the story of Jay.

I would also like to acknowledge Hyerin Moon, Jiyoung Oh, and Michela Mangiaracina at Best Life Media for helping me shape the story through different editing phases. Daniel Graham artfully translated the Korean story into English, and Jack Forem added joyful rhythms to the story with his thoughtful editing. Thank you as well to the many individuals who helped to improve the English translation after its first printing.

My gratitude also goes to Michael Munson, who lent his inspirational voice for the guided meditation CD, and to Kenny Star, who mixed and edited the tracks.

ABOUT JISU HAN

Jisu Han is an accomplished illustrator who has worked on various children's books, adult fables, and inspirational books. All of her illustrations are hand painted using various media.

Jisu's meditations on the bird of her soul and the personal growth she gained from them made her the perfect choice for this project. Her soul connection inspired and informed her work throughout the creative process.

Jisu dreams of a world in which the souls of all people are awakened and all life-forms dance together in oneness. She desires to express that world in her illustrations.

ABOUT ILCHI LEE

Ilchi Lee is an impassioned visionary, educator, mentor, and innovator; he has dedicated his life not only to teaching energy principles, but also to researching and developing methods to nurture the full potential of the human brain.

For over thirty years, his life's mission has been to empower people and to help them harness their own creative power and personal potential. To enable individuals to achieve that goal, he has developed many successful mind–body training methods, including Dahn Yoga and Brain Education. His principles and methods have inspired millions of people around the world to live healthier and happier lives.

Lee is a *New York Times* bestselling author who has penned thirty-five books, including *The Call of Sedona: Journey of the Heart, Change: Realizing Your Greatest Potential,* and *Brain Wave Vibration: Getting Back into the Rhythm of a Happy, Healthy Life.*

He is also a well-respected humanitarian who has been working with the United Nations and other organizations for global peace. Lee serves as the president of the University of Brain Education and the International Brain Education Association. For more information about Ilchi Lee and his work, visit www.ilchi.com.